CHERI

LIVING THE *Message* OF LIGHT:

God's Love

Poems of Praise
FOR GOD'S ETERNAL
LIGHT IN OUR LIVES

Outskirts Press, Inc.
http://www.outskirtspress.com

ISBN: 978-1-4787-8834-8

Outskirts Press and the "OP" logo are trademarks belonging to Outskirts Press, Inc.

PRINTED IN THE UNITED STATES OF AMERICA

Introduction:

My job is to tell people about Jesus. Let his light shine through you in all that you do. Be a reflection of his light. Do it to the best of your ability because the best is who you are. Live the written Word and share it with others. Tell people about your love for Jesus. Spread his message to everyone who will listen. People who are already saved do not need to be saved again; they already have a place in Heaven. Find the ones who are lost, walking out of the light in the darkness. Tell them about the light, God's love, show them, and share his Word. The only way to get the message out there is to be the message. Let God's love be shown in all that you do!

My Gift:

God communicates to my spirit and I am able to write his words down to share them with the world. God uses me for a healing ministry for the world that is lost.

Contents

The Price

Your body paid the price for our sins
You gladly laid down your life
For all mankind to live again
With your blood you cleansed us all
Thank you, Jesus, for loving us all.

Child of Mine

You sent your son to die for me
Your only child so that we could be free
He walked among us as a man
He spoke your words but yet he was condemned
He laid down his life with no fear
So that we could survive
And know that his spirit is Alive!

My Savior

You are my savior
My King
My prince of peace
The one whom I know I can always trust
The one I can confide in
The one I can hide in
My fortress
My protector
My shield of Faith.

Jesus

Many times I have heard your voice,
Many times I have not listened,
But still you spoke to me,
And directed me in how to be free,
One day I stopped and listened,
The voice that I heard spoke a solid word,
And it cried at my heart's door,
I welcomed the words that my heart heard,
And I opened my soul to you,
I welcomed you in and you freed me from sin,
Now every day we walk and pray.

Untitled

You were always with me in times of need,
You never left me, for I was your seed,
You watched me grow and let me choose my own way,
But you came to me and presented yourself again,
And I chose to follow you until the very end.

A Place for Me

I have faith in the day and the night,
I have faith in the stars in the sky,
I have faith in my creator,
For you created all that was or will ever be,
I believe in my Lord and Savior,
And I know that he is preparing a place for me in Eternity!

Walking with the Son

Oh, little children, how strong your faith will be,
As strong as I while you are abiding in me,
When all were created our walks were as one,
And know again we can walk with the Son.

Untitled

When they rolled the stone away
from the tomb on that third day,
It was as empty as before,
But when they looked outside the tomb,
Jesus appeared in spirit form,
The body of the man had gone away,
And Jesus himself was of new body,
You gave up your life for all humanity,
So that we could all be free.

The Cross

The cross is a symbol,
That reminds me of what my savior did for me,
You laid down your life so I could be free,
Free from a life of uncertainty,
You came in the form of man,
So that I could understand,
You left behind a legacy,
Through your word we may know you,
And through our lives we may show you.

My Jesus

My savior, my father, my friend,
You created me and let me live,
You gave me the right to choose my own way,
But somehow we got lost,
So you sent your son to save the day,
My life was meaningless,
And yours was blessed,
Mine led me astray,
Yours led me the right way,
You showed me a love that can only be found in heaven above,
You gave me hope, a reason to live life,
You are my savior,
You are my Jesus Christ!

Untitled

My King, the first in command,
My leader, my father, my friend,
You gave your son so that all men could be free,
But some were blinded by the love you had for me,
You laid down your life at Calvary,
So that I could live and be free,
The only thing you wanted in return,
Was for me to know you, to live and to learn,
You set me free so that I could tell people of your ways,
So we could all love and praise you.

Mighty

Mighty is a word that means strong and brave,
Mighty is our King, who knows our thoughts and ways,
Mighty is the one who takes away all fear,
Mighty is the one who dwells within our soul,
Mighty is the shield that he upholds,
Mighty is the Lord for all he has done,
Mighty is Jesus, the father's son.

Untitled

Sometimes when I was all alone my mind, it started to wonder,
Then one day I realized that we are never alone,
That God is always listening,
He is always with us by our side,
He never leaves us and never hides,
So then I knew in my thoughts that this was
how I was praying!

Praying

Prayer is an emotion,
Something that your spirit does,
It's a conversation that you have with God,
He will always answer you,
Even when you might not be willing to listen,
Next time you are wondering what the message is,
Pay close attention to be listening,
So you don't miss out on your blessings.

Past-Present-Future

Past- My God created me…
Present- Molding me into his likeness…
Future- What I will be in him…

Past- Our old ways
Present- Our new life / ways
Future- How to please God, to live for him,
To be more like him!

Past- Then / Present- Now / Future- Eternity

Heaven's Gate

Our soul is a door that leads us to Heaven's Gate
The choice is ours to make,
For me the choice is clear,
I choose life and to live it with no fear,
But for some they choose to shut the gate,
And seal their fate,
But for many they live in the light,
The path they have taken has opened the gate,
Glorious treasures and a wonderful King,
Greet them each morning and are with them all day,
While they worship in spirit and praise.

Keeper of the Light

The keeper of the light is not selfish in any way,
In fact he just keeps giving it away!
It's all around us,
It's in everything we see and do,
It shields us from the world around,
And leads us to solid ground,
It has love, hope, and faith,
Its face has never been seen,
But it is heard often throughout the day,
The light is bright and it glows in an immaculate way,
It is our soul, our creator,
It is the only way!

My God

In my weakest and darkest hour,
You protect me when I cower,
I feel ashamed and frightened,
But you hide me,
You take pride in me,
You carry me through,
And make my spirit feel brand-new!
You are my protector, my helper,
And again when I am sad,
You cheer me up and make me glad!

The Answer

My heart sings a song and my body dances to the beat,
It sings hallelujah, hallelujah, the good Lord has called,
And I answer in awe,
He must be able to depend on me,
I will let him use me to do his will,
This is the answer he has revealed!

Promise Keeper

You are the promise keeper,
The one who never lies,
You stand by your Word,
And always lend and ear to what needs to be heard,
Always faithful and just to forgive,
I am only a child and you are so big,
I have my ways but you have your will,
I choose to follow you,
I choose to fulfill.

Change My Ways

My ways are not your ways,
My will is not your will,
My thoughts are my thoughts,
And my life stands still,
So I ask you to change my ways,
To make me more like you,
To change my will so I can see the good,
In all that people do,
Take my thoughts,
Mold me oh, Lord,
Have your way in me.

Take Control

Sometimes I go to a place where I might never go,
I feel odd at first but I know I am never alone,
You lead me to step out of place,
But always you are there showing your face,
I speak boldly to people I don't know,
You take me out of my place,
And put me in yours,
You take control.

Live in His Love

My God has supplied for all my needs,
From the very small to the very large,
It's really a matter of simple faith,
Nothing is too big for our Lord,
All of our gifts have already been given to us,
It's all in how we live our life,
And what we believe in,
Our Lord in heaven has blessed us so much,
All we need to do is live in His Love.

Abiding in God's Love

Our lives have many directions that they can go,
One path may lead to worry,
One path may lead to hate,
One path will lead to Heaven's gate,
The road will be rocky and sometimes seem long,
But on this path you are not alone,
For greater is He that is in you,
Than he that is in the world,
God will give you all your heart desires,
And when you have lived long and are satisfied,
You will join Him in Heaven's Glory.

Direction

The road is long and the journey very hard,
My struggles great and the fear strong,
My ways have led me all the wrong directions,
And now I am at a dead end,
I give up, Lord, and want to go your direction,
Take your ways and make them mine,
Lead me in your direction,
Provide me with protection.

You Choose Me

My way is not His way, my will is not His will,
I go my own way, I travel my own road,
The path I have taken is not the one you chose,
My heart is breaking and my life goes nowhere,
But always beside me you where there is guild me,
Always wanting to provide for me and set me free,
Oh Lord, so strong, Oh me, so weak,
You gave me hope and eternity,
My way is your way, my will is your will,
My life belongs to you,
My path is your path, I choose to follow you, oh Lord,
My life has meaning, purpose and faith,
For you choose me, oh Lord, to share something great.

Forgiven

You are my safe place, my refuge,
You protect me and forgive all my wrongs,
No matter what the mistakes great or small,
You write them off and forgive them all,
You comfort me in times of need,
You encourage me when it need be,
But most of all you set me free!

Control Me

There is never any problem that you cannot fix,
When I am in need you always have an answer,
You fill me with your love and mercy and
guide me to the answer,
My problems have been great and very small,
You were always listening,
Knowing what I needed most of all,
I opened my heart and you filled my spirit,
You took control in me,
So that I could live with you in eternity.

You Were Always There

You were always beside me, there to guide me,
Always wanting to provide for me,
You never left me alone,
Our paths were always one,
Whenever I felt scared or sad,
You lit my path and made me glad,
You taught me how to feel no fear,
And how to live according to your will.

Destiny

In my hour of need you are always there,
You have never left me and have always cared,
When I was weak you made me strong,
When the day felt long, like it was never going to end,
You gave me hope,
No matter how bad life seemed to get,
You offered me freedom with no regret,
You showed me that there was always light
at the end of the tunnel,
And always you were there with me,
So that I could fulfill my destiny.

Your Way

When I am alone, sad, and lost,
You pick me up,
Just like when you carried the cross,
You died for me and all my sins,
You paid the price so that I could live again,
You helped me get through each day,
And guided me in your ways,
You teach me how to be more like you,
And always listen when I am confused,
You hold my hand and lead me through each day,
Thank you, God, for helping me live life your way!

Untitled

You are my savior,
Lord of all,
You created all things great and small,
From the tiniest ant to the whales in the sea,
You made all this world for me!

My King

You are the King of Kings,
The Prince of peace,
My Savior and my best friend,
You taught me how to live again,
In my hour of uncertain faith,
You came to me and showed me grace,
When I was weak you made me strong,
You protected me and brought me home.

Me First

You have always thought of me first,
Even though sometimes I thought of you last,
You made sure that my past didn't matter,
You sent your son so that I could be free,
By the shedding of his blood on Calvary,
You prepared a place for me in Heaven,
You left us your Word for direction,
You always thought of me first,
Even before I was here,
So I think of you often,
And I know that you are here.

Children

Beauty can be found in the face of a child,
The ears of the children hear what we may not,
Their eyes see with an innocence,
That is lost when we are old,
But with age comes wisdom, knowledge, and faith,
Children learn from what they see,
And as they grow they need eternity,
So teach them well the ways of the Lord,
So they may grow and stay in the Word!

Love

Love one another as He has loved you,
He gave up His only Son,
So you could be renewed,
Giving us hope,
So that we could be free,
And live for an eternity!

The Light

The light is always present,
Its holds a beauty from within,
It's radiant and shines,
From the Heavens to the Earth,
It dominates all that it touches,
It reaches in and heals your soul,
There is a protection that comes from within,
A comfort in knowing that it is there,
The light has many outlets,
You can use in many ways,
The light is never ending,
It is forever and always.

Rainbow

A rainbow is a symbol to remind us of God's love,
Its colors are bright and vivid,
Everyone knows when it is there,
It can be seen from anywhere,
There is never an end to where it goes,
God's love is never fading,
And bright as the colors in the rainbow,
People around you can see the change in your ways,
Your life has meaning, purpose, and faith,
It is a reflection of God's love and unchanging grace.

Untitled

Through many times and many reasons,
My ways were concurred by my freedom,
I chose to live my life my own way,
Day by day,
I quickly tired and with regret my life became a mess,
You held the answers and the keys,
You knew what I needed was to be free,
You gave me life and proper instructions,
So that my life would not lead to destruction.

Bible

This little book of mine,
It's been around for a long time,
From Old Testament to New,
The story always seems to bring me back to you,
It's got all the answers and all the facts,
Every detail big or small,
Is something you wanted to share with us all!

Untitled

My life it was so empty,
But now it is so full,
You saved me from a life of shame, fear, and regret,
You delivered me from insanity,
You brought me out of poverty,
And made my life what you wanted it to be,
You took pride in me,
You died for me,
You set me free,
You wait for me in eternity!

With Me

I had a vision of what my life should be like,
But nowhere in it did I see Christ,
I thought my life would be complete,
If I had all I ever wanted,
But my way was not the right way,
My will was not His will,
I felt empty and alone,
So Christ gave me a home,
I let Him lead the way,
So everywhere I go,
I will not stray.

Friend in Jesus

People all over the world are hurting,
Their pain comes from within,
A husband, a wife, a grandmother,
All over people are hurt,
Because they have not a friend in Jesus.

His Direction

The world is big and round,
And it rotates from sunup to sundown,
We are always going in circles,
We are always going 'round and 'round,
There is always an up and a down,
If you have your feet firmly planted on the ground,
Your world only goes one direction,
It is a way that many know,
Your feet follow a Savior, a King, Emanuel,
So for me there is only one direction,
And the way I want to go is His direction!

Purpose

God has a purpose and a plan,
Our life is much more than what we demand,
God sent His Son to die for you and me,
So that we could be free,
He gave us our life and let us choose our own way,
He left us a book which contains life's instructions,
If we follow His Word then his voice will be heard!

Love Inside You

Jesus is Lord, a mighty King,
He will end all suffering,
A heart He heals,
A soul He mends,
Jesus is much more than a friend,
He will walk with you, talk with you,
Defend you until the end,
He will provide for you,
Take pride in you,
All you have to do is let His love inside of you.

Lord

You were there when I was conceived,
You planted me in the womb,
You watched me as I grew and kept me close to you,
You taught me how to be blessed,
To share your Word and to confess,
You bring me joy and I honor you,
You keep me safe and I love you.

Your Love

You have always had all the answers,
Even though the questions to us were unknown,
No matter what the problem you could fix it,
You helped me each and every day,
You taught me your ways,
Thank you, Jesus, for sharing your love.

Free

You put the stars in the sky,
And the birds in the air,
You taught me how to love and share,
No matter how big the problems you knew how to solve them,
Always an answer, always a key,
You taught me how to be free.

The Right Road

Life is much more than just you and me,
Life is much better in eternity,
People around you who are not yet saved,
Are souls searching for salvation who have lost their way,
It's our job to prepare them and show them the light,
We must walk with them through the night,
The day will come and the light will grow,
And then they will be on the right road.

Listen

We come from dust and just one breath,
A simple answer but not a simple quest,
Our hearts have been heavy,
Some have had fear,
But to those of you who choose to listen,
Your heart is eased and there is no more fear,
For Jesus is here!

Instructions

I let my spirit tell me what God wants me to do,
I stop, pray, and He leads me to the direction that
He wants me to go,
Sometimes the answer is not clear,
But I always listen to what there is to hear,
I pay attention to the simple instructions,
For not to would lead to my destruction.

Salvation

We confess with our mouths and He is true to say,
That he will fulfill us for all of our days,
No pain is too great, for He carries them all,
No sin is too great that it can build up a wall,
For Jesus is Lord and He came to save us all!

Eternity

You gave me hope and an eternity,
You taught me how to live and be free,
You gave me my life and let me live it,
But you thought of me and showed me forgiveness,
You set me free and showed me eternity.

Earl

Though it took some time, you were forgiven,
Our Lord Jesus was just asking to be let in,
Many a heart has prayed for you,
For your salvation to be true,
My God has delivered you,
All your problems you took to the cross,
And so salvation is not a loss,
Our Lord and Savior saved you.

Don't Cry for Me

Don't cry for me
For I have not gone away from you,
I am still with you,
A piece of me has been left in you,
So that I might live on,
Remember me as I was in the end,
For I found Jesus and He was my friend,
He has guided me in this direction,
And brought me home under His protection.

Never Too Late

Don't be sad for me as my body is at rest,
For my spirit is with the Lord and I am happy and blessed,
It's never too late for your salvation to begin,
What's truly important is your destination in the end.

God's Grace

We are here but for a moment,
A mere fraction in time,
Our place on this earth lasts for just a short time,
Our destiny and what we are to become,
Is a place in eternity seated with the Son,
Though you may question your time on Earth,
Your soul seeks the truth of your birth,
At times you may feel hopeless or a bit out of place,
But eternity offers God's Grace!

My Savior

There is a special way that she carries herself,
A glow from deep within her soul,
Her heart is never heavy or sad,
She takes joy and pride in loving her man,
She seeks after only one thing,
He holds her close and lives in her heart,
Always together and never apart,
Her destiny is only to serve him,
He is more than her father and more than a friend,
He is her provider, King of Kings,
He is her Savior and her beginning.

Someday

There are times when life seems to go nowhere,
Like time just left you standing there,
When hope seems lost and you are in the middle of despair,
Lift up your heart to the man upstairs,
For he is listening to all your cares,
You are destined to meet him someday,
So why not now? Stop and pray.

Near Jesus

I have a book that is very special to me,
The words inside make me come alive and set me free,
They teach me how to live in this world,
And provide me with direction to the next,
The book's pages are worn and I use it often,
It protects me from all fear,
It keeps me safe and brings Jesus near.

Prayer

Prayer is the most powerful message God can hear,
It comes from your soul and is intended only for His ears,
He always answers the prayer of the heart,
All He asks is that you follow His will,
And your way will be fulfilled.

A New Beginning

Today is the day when my life must end,
But in its place a new one will begin,
A heart that was once heavy and weighed down with fear,
Has patience, love, and the future is clear,
Though all the answers may not come at once,
They are surely there and will come with prayer.

Born Again

How to live life when you are born again,
Is really quite simple, my friend,
Once you were lost,
But now have a home,
Your heart is no longer heavy,
And you are no longer alone,
You are filled with a joy and unconditional love,
And no one can take from you what God has ordained
from above.

Closer

My goal is much closer than it was last week,
I feel somewhat stronger as I press on day by day,
My gift is being processed,
And I am surely on my way,
The Lord is using me to share something great!